Tha... you!

THANK YOU FOR
PURCHASING:

LEARN PYTHON
WITH MONSTERS

*A Fun Way to Begin
Programming*

Your support means a lot, and I'm grateful you
chose this book.

Feel free to share any monster python tips you
enjoyed in your review!

Thank you and enjoy.

Python Tip1

The print() function displays the message inside the parentheses.In this case, it will print "Hello, World!" to the console.

```
>print("Hello, World!")
```

To run this code, open a Python interpreter or a Python IDE, paste the code, and execute it. You should see the output "Hello, World!" displayed on the screen.

Congratulations on your first step into Python programming! Keep exploring and enjoy your coding journey!

Addition

Asks the user to input two numbers and then adds them together:

```python
# Input from user
num1 = float(input("Enter the first number: "))
num2 = float(input("Enter the second number: "))

# Addition
result = num1 + num2

# Display the result
print("The sum of", num1, "and", num2, "is:", result)
```

This concise program prompts the user to input two numbers using input(), converts the inputs to floating-point numbers using float(), and then performs addition with the + operator. Finally, it displays the result using print(). The program is kept simple and should easily fit on one page.

P y t h o n   T i p 2

Comment Your Code

Use comments to explain your code and add notes for better understanding.

Comments start with the # symbol and are ignored by the Python interpreter. They are useful for documenting your code and providing explanations for yourself and others who read your code.

```
>print("Hello, World!")
#Output: Hello, World!
```

Basic Calculator

Basic calculator in Python that focuses on subtraction and multiplication:

```python
def subtract(num1, num2):
    return num1 - num2

def multiply(num1, num2):
    return num1 * num2

while True:
    print("Basic Calculator")
    print("1. Subtract")
    print("2. Multiply")
    print("3. Exit")

    choice = input("Enter choice (1/2/3): ")

    if choice == '1':
        num1 = float(    "Enter the first number: ")
        num2 = float(    "Enter the second number: ")
        print(f"Result: {subtract(num1, num2)}")
    elif choice == '2':
        num1 = float(    "Enter the first number: ")
        num2 = float(    "Enter the second number: ")
        print(f"Result: {multiply(num1, num2)}")
    elif choice == '3':
        print("Goodbye!")
        break
    else:
        print("Invalid choice. Please select again.")
```

Python Tip3

Use len() to Get the Length of a String or List

The len() function in Python is used to find the length of a string or a list. It returns the number of characters in a string or the number of elements in a list.

Example 1 - Using len() with a string:

```
> text="Hello, World!"
> length_of_text = len(text)
> print(length_of_text) # Output:13
```

Example 2 - Using len() with a list:

```
> numbers = [1, 2, 3, 4, 5]
> length_of_numbers = len(numbers)
> print(length_of_numbers) # Output:5
```

Counting

A small Python program that counts from 1 to 10 using a loop:

```python
# Counting from 1 to 10

# Using a for loop
for number in range(1, 11):
    print(number)
```

<u>output:</u>

```
1
2
3
4
5
6
7
8
9
10
```

This program uses a for loop with the range function. The range(1, 11) generates a sequence of numbers from 1 to 10 (including 1 but excluding 11). The loop iterates over this sequence, and print(number) displays the numbers from 1 to 10 on separate lines.

Python Tip 4

Using input() to Get User Input

The input() function in Python allows you to take input from the user during the execution of your program. It waits for the user to enter a value and press the Enter key, and then it returns the entered value as a string.

```
>name = input("Enter your name: ")
>print("Hello, " + name + "! Nice to meet you!")
```

When this code is executed, it will prompt the user to enter their name. Whatever the user enters will be stored in the variable name, and the program will greet them with a personalized message.

Output:

Enter your name: John
Hello, John! Nice to meet you!

Drawing

A program that allows the user to draw a square using the Turtle graphics library:

```python
# Drawing a Square with Turtle
import turtle

# Function to draw a square
def draw_square():
    for _ in range(4):
        turtle.forward(100)
        turtle.right(90)

# Main program
if __name__ == "__main__":
    turtle.speed(1)  # Set turtle
speed (1 = slowest, 10 = fastest)

    draw_square()

    turtle.done()

# Finish the drawing
```

output:

The program runs and a square is drawn on the screen using the Turtle graphics library.

Try and draw a circle now.

hint:
```python
def draw_circle():
        turtle.circle(50)
```

P y t h o n   T i p 5

Data Types in Python

In Python, data types represent the different kinds of data that can be used in your programs. Here are some common data types:

1. Integers: Whole numbers without decimal points, such as '42' or '-10'.
2. Floats: Numbers with decimal points, such as '3.14' or '-0.5'.
3. Strings: Sequences of characters, enclosed in single or double quotes, like '"hello"' or '"Python"'.
4. Booleans: Logical values that can be either True or False.

Understanding data types is crucial as it helps you work with different kinds of data and perform operations based on their characteristics. Happy coding!

Even or Odd

A small program for that checks if a given number is even or odd:

```python
# Even or Odd

# Input from user
number = int(input("Enter a number: "))

# Check if the number is even or odd
if number % 2 == 0:
    print(number, "is an even number.")
else:
    print(number, "is an odd number.")
```

<u>output:</u>

```
Enter a number: 9
9 is an odd number.
```

In this program, we use the modulo operator % to check if the remainder of dividing the input number by 2 is equal to 0. If it is, then the number is even; otherwise, it is odd. The program then displays the result accordingly.

P y t h o n   T i p 6

Basic Arithmetic in Python

Python supports standard arithmetic operations for numbers:

- Addition: +
- Subtraction: -
- Multiplication: *
- Division: /
- Integer Division: //
- Modulo (Remainder): %
- Exponentiation: **

```
x = 5 y = 2
sum_result = x + y
difference_result = x - y
product_result = x * y
division_result = x / y
integer_division_result = x // y
remainder_result = x % y
exponent_result = x ** y
print(sum_result, difference_result,
product_result)
print(division_result, integer_division_result,
remainder_result, exponent_result)
```

output:

7 3 10 2.5 2 1 25

Fibonacci

A small Python program that generates the first few numbers in the Fibonacci sequence:

```python
# Input from user
terms = int(input("Enter the number of Fibonacci terms to generate: "))

# First two terms of the sequence
num1, num2 = 0, 1

# Check if the number of terms is valid
if terms <= 0:
    print("Please enter a positive integer.")
elif terms == 1:
    print("Fibonacci sequence:")
    print(num1)
else:
    print("Fibonacci sequence:")
    print(num1, ",", num2, end=", ")
    for _ in range(2, terms):
        next_num = num1 + num2
        print(next_num, end=", ")
        num1, num2 = num2, next_num

print()  # To add a new line after the sequence is printed
```

In this program, we take the number of Fibonacci terms to generate as input from the user. We then use a for loop to calculate and print the Fibonacci sequence up to the specified number of terms.

Python Tip7

Operator Precedence

When using multiple operators in an expression, Python follows operator precedence rules to determine the order of evaluation. Here's the general order, from highest to lowest precedence:

1. Parentheses ( ): Operations inside parentheses are evaluated first.
2. Exponentiation **: Exponents are evaluated next.
3. Multiplication *, Division /, Integer Division //, and Modulo %: These are evaluated from left to right.
4. Addition + and Subtraction - : These are evaluated from left to right.

```
result = 2 + 3 * 4
print(result) # Output: 14
```

In this example, **3 * 4** is evaluated first (giving **12**), then **2 + 12** is evaluated, resulting in **14**.

~~~~~~

```
result = (2 + 3) * 4
print(result) # Output: 20
```

In this case, **(2 + 3)** is evaluated first (giving **5**), and then **5 * 4** results in **20**.

Guessing Game

A small Python program for a simple guessing game where the user has to guess a secret number:

```python
import random

secret_number = random.randint(1, 100)

attempts = 5

print("Welcome to the Guessing Game!")
print(f"Guess the secret number between
1 and 100. You have {attempts}
attempts.")

# Main game loop
for attempt in range(1, attempts + 1):
    guess = int(input("Enter your guess:
"))

    if guess == secret_number:
        print("Congratulations! You
guessed the correct number!")
        break
    elif guess < secret_number:
        print("Too low! Try again.")
    else:
        print("Too high! Try again.")

    attempts_left = attempts - attempt
    if attempts_left > 0:
        print(f"You have {attempts_left}
{'attempts' if attempts_left > 1 else
'attempt'} left.")
    else:
        print("Out of attempts! The
secret number was", secret_number)
```

In this program, a secret number between 1 and 100 is generated randomly using the **random.randint()** function. The user has 5 attempts to guess the number correctly.

Python Tip 8

Conditional Statements in Python

Conditional statements allow you to make decisions in your code based on certain conditions. They use the keywords if, else, and elif (short for "else if").

```
x = 10
if x > 0:
    print("x is positive")
elif x == 0:
    print("x is zero")
else:
    print("x is negative")
```

output:

x is positive

In this example, the program checks the value of **x** and executes the corresponding block of code based on the condition:

- If **x > 0**, it prints "x is positive."
- If **x == 0**, it prints "x is zero."
- If none of the above conditions are true, it prints "x is negative."

Hangman

A small Python program for a simple Hangman game where the user guesses letters to complete a word:

```python
import random

words = ["apple", "banana", "cherry",
"orange", "grape", "watermelon"]
word = random.choice(words)
guessed_letters = ["_"] * len(word)
attempts = 6

print(" ".join(guessed_letters))

while attempts > 0 and "_" in
guessed_letters:
    guess = input("Enter a letter: ")
    if guess in word:
        for i, letter in
enumerate(word):
            if letter == guess:
                guessed_letters[i] =
guess
    else:
        attempts -= 1
        print(f"Incorrect guess.
Attempts left: {attempts}")

    print(" ".join(guessed_letters))

if "_" not in guessed_letters:
    print("Congratulations! You guessed
the word correctly!")
else:
    print(f"Out of attempts! The word
was {word}")
```

In this program, a list of words is provided for the game, and a random word is selected from the list. The user has 6 attempts to guess letters that appear in the word.

Python Tip 9

Loops in Python

Loops allow you to repeat a block of code multiple times. There are two main types of loops in Python:

- **for Loop**: It iterates over a sequence (e.g., a list, string, or range) and executes the block of code for each item in the sequence.

```python
fruits = ["apple", "banana", "cherry"]
for fruit in fruits:
        print(fruit)
```

output:
```
apple
banana
cherry
```

- **while Loop**: It repeats the block of code as long as a certain condition is true.

```python
count = 1
while count <= 3:
        print("Hello")
        count += 1
```

output:
```
Hello
Hello
Hello
```

Input Validation

A small Python program for "Input Validation" that validates user input to ensure it's a positive integer:

```python
while True:
    user_input = input("Enter a positive integer: ")

    if user_input.isdigit():
        number = int(user_input)
        if number > 0:
            break
        else:
            print("Please enter a positive integer.")
    else:
        print("Invalid input. Please enter a positive integer.")

print(f"You entered: {number}")
```

In this program, we use a while loop to repeatedly prompt the user to enter a value until a valid positive integer is provided. The isdigit() method is used to check if the user input consists only of digits (i.e., a positive integer). If the input is a positive integer, the loop is broken, and the program proceeds. If the input is not a positive integer, the user is prompted to try again.

Python Tip10

Lists in Python

Lists are ordered collections of items in Python. They can contain elements of different data types and are mutable, meaning you can add, remove, or modify elements in a list:

```
fruits = ["apple", "banana",
"cherry"] print(fruits)
```

output:
```
["apple", "banana", "cherry"]
```

You can access elements in a list using index numbers, where the first element has index 0 (which would be apple in the below example):

```
fruits = ["apple", "banana",
"cherry"] print(fruits[1])
```

output:
```
banana
```

Lists are versatile and commonly used in Python for storing and manipulating data.

Joke Generator

Here's a small Python program for a "Joke Generator" that randomly selects and displays a joke from a list of jokes:

```python
# Joke Generator

import random

jokes = [
    "Why don't scientists trust atoms? Because they make up everything!",
    "What do you call fake spaghetti? An impasta!",
    "Why don't some couples go to the gym? Because some relationships don't work out!",
    "Why did the scarecrow win an award? Because he was outstanding in his field!",
    "Why don't skeletons fight each other? They don't have the guts!",
]

# Select a random joke from the list
random_joke = random.choice(jokes)

print("Here's a joke for you:")
print(random_joke)
```

In this program, we have a list of jokes stored in the jokes variable. The program uses the random.choice() function to select a random joke from the list. It then displays the selected joke to the user.

Python Tip11

String Manipulation in Python

String manipulation allows you to work with and modify text data in Python. Here are some common operations you can perform on strings:

- Concatenation: Combine strings using the + operator.

```
greeting = "Hello, "
name = "John"
message = greeting + name
print(message)
```

output:
```
Hello, John
```

- Slicing: Extract parts of a string using slicing notation [start:end].

```
text = "Python is fun"
substring = text[0:6]
print(substring)
```

output:
```
Python
```

String manipulation is essential for working with textual data, and Python provides a wide range of methods to make it easy.

Keyboard Art

A simple program that generates an ACSII art picture:

```python
import random

def draw_random_art():
    art_list = [
        r"""
 /\_/\
( o.o )
 > ^ <
""",
        r"""
 /\_/\
( x.x )
 > ^ <
""",
        # Add more ASCII art images here
    ]
    return random.choice(art_list)

def main():
    print("Press any key to see a random ASCII art.")
    print("Press Q to quit.")

    while True:
        key = input()

        if key.lower() == "q":
            break

        print(draw_random_art())

if __name__ == "__main__":
    main()
```

With this program, each time the user presses any key (except Q), the program will randomly select one of the ASCII art images from the art_list and display it on the screen.

Python Tip12

Functions in Python

Functions are reusable blocks of code that perform specific tasks. They help you organize your code, avoid repetition, and make it more maintainable:

```python
def greet(name):
    print("Hello, " + name + "!")

greet("Alice") # Output:"Hello, Alice!"

greet("Bob")  # Output:"Hello, Bob!"
```

output:
Hello, Alice!
Hello, Bob!

In this example, we defined a function greet() that takes a parameter name and prints a personalized greeting. By calling the function with different names, we can reuse the code block to greet multiple people.

Functions are essential for writing clean and modular code. They allow you to encapsulate logic and make your code easier to read and maintain.

Leap Year

Here's a Python program that checks if a given year is a leap year or not:

```python
def is_leap_year(year):
    if year % 4 == 0:
        if year % 100 == 0:
            if year % 400 == 0:
                return True
            else:
                return False
        else:
            return True
    else:
        return False
def main():
    print("Enter a year to check if it's a leap year:")
    try:
        year = int(input())
        if is_leap_year(year):
            print(f"{year} is a leap year.")
        else:
            print(f"{year} is not a leap year.")
    except ValueError:
        print("Invalid input. Please enter a valid year.")

if __name__ == "__main__":
    main()
```

This program defines a function is_leap_year that takes a year as input and returns True if it's a leap year and False otherwise. It uses the rules for leap years: if a year is divisible by 4 but not by 100, it's a leap year. If a year is divisible by both 4 and 100, it's a leap year only if it's also divisible by 400.

The main function takes user input for the year and then calls the is_leap_year function to check if it's a leap year or not. It then displays the result on the screen.

Python Tip13

Dictionaries in Python

Dictionaries are a data structure that store data in key-value pairs. They allow you to map unique keys to their corresponding values:

```python
student_scores = {"Alice": 85, "Bob": 92, "Charlie": 78}
print(student_scores["Bob"])
```

output:
92

In this example, we have a dictionary student_scores that maps student names to their respective scores. You can access the value associated with a specific key, such as "Bob," by using square brackets with the key (student_scores["Bob"]).

Dictionaries are powerful for efficient data retrieval based on unique keys and are commonly used in various applications.

Multiplication Table

Here's a Python program that displays the multiplication table for a given number:

```python
def multiplication_table(number):
    print(f"Multiplication Table for {number}:")
    for i in range(1, 11):
        print(f"{number} x {i} = {number * i}")

def main():
    print("Enter a number to generate its multiplication table:")
    try:
        number = int(input())
        multiplication_table(number)
    except ValueError:
        print("Invalid input. Please enter a valid number.")

if __name__ == "__main__":
    main()
```

When you run this program, it will ask you to enter a number. After entering the number, it will display the multiplication table for that number from 1 to 10.

Output:

```
Enter a number to generate its multiplication table:
5
Multiplication Table for 5:
5 x 1 = 5
5 x 2 = 10
~
5 x 9 = 45
5 x 10 = 50
```

Python Tip14

Tuples in Python

Tuples are immutable data structures in Python, meaning their elements cannot be changed after creation:

```
person_info = ("Alice", 30, "New York")
print(person_info)
```

output:

```
("Alice", 30, "New York")
```

In this example, we have a tuple person_info containing information about a person: name, age, and location. Once a tuple is created, you cannot modify its elements.

Tuples are useful when you want to create a collection of items that should remain constant throughout the program's execution.

Remember, if you need a data structure that can be modified, use lists; if you need an unchangeable structure, use tuples.

Number Guessing

Here's a Python program for the Number Guessing game:

```python
import random

def number_guessing_game():
    secret_number = random.randint(1,
100)
    attempts = 0

    print("Guess a number between 1 and
100.")

    while True:
        try:
            guess = int(input("Enter
your guess: "))
            attempts += 1

            if guess == secret_number:

 print(f"Congratulations! You guessed
the number {secret_number} in
{attempts} attempts.")
                break
            elif guess < secret_number:
                print("Too low. Try
again.")
            else:
                print("Too high. Try
again.")
        except ValueError:
            print("Invalid input.
Please enter a valid number.")

if __name__ == "__main__":
    number_guessing_game()
```

This generates a random number between 1
and 100, asks the user to guess the number,
and provides feedback based on whether the
guess is too high or too low.

Python Tip 15

Sets in Python

Sets are unordered collections of unique elements in Python. They automatically remove duplicate values, ensuring that each element appears only once in the set:

```python
fruits = {"apple", "banana", "cherry", "apple"}
print(fruits)
```

output:

```
{"apple", "banana", "cherry"}
```

In this example, we have a set fruits containing four elements, including two occurrences of "apple." However, when printed, the set contains only unique elements, and duplicates are automatically removed.

Sets are helpful when you want to work with distinct elements, perform mathematical set operations (e.g., union, intersection), or remove duplicates from a list.

Odd or Even Sum

Here's a Python program for the Odd or Even Sum task:

```python
def odd_even_sum(start, end):
    odd_sum = 0
    even_sum = 0

    for num in range(start, end + 1):
        if num % 2 == 0:
            even_sum += num
        else:
            odd_sum += num

    return odd_sum, even_sum

def main():
    start = int(input("Enter the
starting number: "))
    end = int(input("Enter the ending
number: "))

    odd_sum, even_sum =
odd_even_sum(start, end)

    print(f"Sum of odd numbers between
{start} and {end}: {odd_sum}")
    print(f"Sum of even numbers between
{start} and {end}: {even_sum}")

if __name__ == "__main__":
    main()
```

When you run this program, it will prompt
you to enter the starting and ending
numbers of the range. Then, it will calculate
and display the sum of odd numbers and
even numbers separately within that range.

File Handling in Python

File handling allows you to read from and write to files on your computer. It enables interaction with external data, such as reading text from a file or saving program output to a file:

Writing to a File:

```python
with open("example.txt", "w") as file:
    file.write("Hello, world!\n")
    file.write("This is a sample file.")
```

Reading from a File:

```python
with open("example.txt", "r") as file:
    content = file.read()
    print(content)
```

In the first example, we open a file named "example.txt" in write mode ("w") and write some text into it.

In the second example, we open the same file in read mode ("r") and read its content into the content variable. Then, we print the content of the file.

File handling is crucial for data processing, data storage, and interacting with external resources in Python.

Prime Numbers

Here's a Python program that checks if a given number is prime or not:

```python
def            number :
    if number <= 1:
        return False
    for i in range(2, int(number**0.5) +
1):
        if number % i == 0:
            return False
    return True

def main():
    num = int(input("Enter a number: "))

    if            num :
        print(f"{num} is a prime
number.")
    else:
        print(f"{num} is not a prime
number.")

if __name__ == "__main__":
    main()
```

This program defines a function is_prime that takes a number as input and checks if it is a prime number or not. The function returns True if the number is prime, and False otherwise.

In the **main** function, the user is prompted to enter a number, and the program calls the   function to determine if the entered number is prime or not.

Note: A prime number is a number greater than 1 that has no divisors other than 1 and itself. Example: 2, 3, 5.

Python Tip17

Importing Modules in Python

Python allows you to import external modules, which are pre-written libraries of code, to extend the functionality of your programs:

```python
# Import the math module to access mathematical functions
import math
# Using the math module to calculate the square root
result = math.sqrt(25)
print(result)
```

output:
5.0

In this example, we import the **math** module, which provides various mathematical functions, and then use it to calculate the square root of 25.

By importing modules, you can access a wide range of pre-built functionality without having to write the code yourself. Python has a rich ecosystem of modules, making it a powerful language for various applications.

Quiz Game

Here's a simple Python program for a quiz game:

```python
def quiz_game():
    questions = [
        ("What is the capital of France?", "Paris"),
        ("Which planet is closest to the Sun?", "Mercury"),
        # Add more questions and answers here
    ]

    score = 0

    print("Welcome to the Quiz Game!")
    print("Please type your answer.")
    print("Let's get started!")

    for question, answer in questions:
        print(question)
        user_answer = input("Your answer: ")

        if user_answer.lower() == answer.lower():
            print("Correct!\n")
            score += 1
        else:
            print(f"Sorry, the correct answer was: {answer}\n")

    print(f"Your final score is: {score} out of {len(questions)}")

if __name__ == "__main__":
    quiz_game()
```

The user's answer is compared to the correct answer, and the program prints whether the answer is correct or not. The final score is displayed at the end.

Python Tip18

Exception Handling in Python

Exception handling allows you to deal with errors gracefully by providing alternative code paths when unexpected issues occur:

```python
try:
    num1 = int(input("Enter a number: "))
    num2 = int(input("Enter another number: "))
    result = num1 / num2
    print("Result:", result)
except ValueError:
    print("Please enter valid integers.")
except ZeroDivisionError:
    print("Cannot divide by zero.")
```

output:
Enter a number:

In this example, the code tries to perform a division operation based on user input. However, if the user provides invalid input (e.g., non-integer values) or attempts to divide by zero, exceptions (ValueError and ZeroDivisionError) may occur.

Using the **try-except** block, we catch these exceptions and execute alternative code blocks to handle the errors gracefully. It prevents the program from crashing and allows you to display helpful error messages to users.

Random Facts

Here's a simple Python program for a random fact generator:

```python
import random

def random_facts():
    facts_list = [
        "The Eiffel Tower can be 15 cm
taller during the summer.",
        "Rats can't vomit.",
        "Honey never spoils.
Archaeologists have found pots of honey
in ancient Egyptian tombs that are over
3,000 years old and still edible.",
        "The average person will spend
six months of their life waiting for red
lights to turn green.",
        # Add more fun facts here
    ]

    print("Welcome to the Random Facts
Generator!")
    print("Press Enter to get a random
fun fact.")
    print("Press Q to quit.")

    while True:
        key = input()

        if key.lower() == "q":
            break

        print(random.choice(facts_list))

if __name__ == "__main__":
```

This program will display random fun facts
from the facts_list each time the user
presses Enter, and it will continue until the
user presses Q to quit the program.

List Comprehensions in Python

List comprehensions offer a concise and elegant way to create lists in a single line of code, allowing you to perform operations on elements from an existing list:

```python
# Using a list comprehension to
create a list of squares
numbers = [1, 2, 3, 4, 5]
squares = [num**2 for num in
numbers]
print(squares)
```

output:

```
[1, 4, 9, 16, 25]
```

In this example, we use a list comprehension to create a new list squares containing the squares of each element in the numbers list.

The list comprehension syntax **[expression for item in list]** allows you to apply the **expression** to each **item** in the **list**, generating a new list based on the result.

List comprehensions are powerful tools to streamline your code and make it more readable. They are particularly useful when you need to transform or filter elements in a list.

String Manipulation

Here's a simple program that asks the user for a string and performs basic string operations:

```python
def string_manipulation():
    user_input = input("Enter a string: ")

    # Reverse the string
    reversed_string = user_input[::-1]
    print("Reversed string:", reversed_string)

    # Convert the string to uppercase
    uppercase_string = user_input.upper()
    print("Uppercase string:", uppercase_string)

    # Convert the string to lowercase
    lowercase_string = user_input.lower()
    print("Lowercase string:", lowercase_string)

if __name__ == "__main__":
    string_manipulation()
```

Output:
```
Enter a string:  monster
('Reversed string:', 'retsnom')
('Uppercase string:', 'MONSTER')
('Lowercase string:', 'monster')
```

When you run this program, it will prompt you to enter a string. After entering the string, it will display the reversed version of the string, as well as the uppercase and lowercase versions of the input string.

Python Tip 20

Randomness in Python

Python provides a built-in random module that allows you to work with random numbers, make random choices, and shuffle sequences:

```python
import random
# Generating a random integer
between 1 and 10 (inclusive)
random_number = random.randint(1,
10) print(random_number) # Output:
(e.g., 7)
```

output:
Any number 1 to 10

```python
import random
fruits = ["apple", "banana",
"cherry", "orange"]
random_fruit = random.choice(fruits)
print(random_fruit) # Output: (e.g.,
"banana")
```

output:
Any fruit in list above

In these examples, we use the random module to generate random numbers or make random choices from a list. This can be useful for various applications like games, simulations, and randomized algorithms.

Times Tables Quiz

Here's a simple program for a Times Tables Quiz:

```python
import random

def times_tables_quiz():
    print("Welcome to the Times Tables Quiz!")
    score = 0

    for i in range(5):    # You can change the number of questions here
        num1 = random.randint(1, 10)
        num2 = random.randint(1, 10)
        answer = num1 * num2

        user_input = int(input(f"What is {num1} times {num2}? "))

        if user_input == answer:
            print("Correct!")
            score += 1
        else:
            print(f"Wrong! The correct answer is {answer}.")

    print(f"Your score: {score}/5")

if __name__ == "__main__":
    times_tables_quiz()
```

This program will ask the user 5 multiplication questions, each with two random numbers between 1 and 10. The user needs to input the correct answer, and the program will provide feedback after each question. At the end of the quiz, it will display the user's score.

Python Tip 21

Scope and Variables in Python

In Python, variables have different scopes that determine where they can be accessed and modified within a program.

Local variable:

```python
def my_function():
    x = 10 # Local variable x
    print(x)
my_function() # Output: 10
print(x) # Raises NameError: 'x' is
not defined
```

output:
```
10
Error
```

Global Variable:
```python
y = 20 # Global variable y
def my_function():
    print(y) # Accessing the global
variable y
my_function() # Output: 20
print(y) # Output: 20
```

output:
```
20
20
```

In this example, y is defined outside the function, making it a global variable. It can be accessed and used both inside and outside the function. Understanding variable scope is crucial for writing maintainable and bug-free code.

User Input

Here's a simple program that takes user input for their name and age and displays a personalized message:

```python
import datetime

def main():
    name = input("What is your name? ")
    age = int(input("How old are you? "))

    current_year = datetime.datetime.now().year
    birth_year = current_year - age

    print(f"Hello, {name}! You are {age} years old.")
    print(f"You were born in the year {birth_year}.")

if __name__ == "__main__":
    main()
```

Output:
```
What is your name?
Bob
How old are you?

Hello, Bob! You are 22 years old. You were born in the year 2001.
```

When you run this program, it will prompt the user to enter their name and age. After receiving the inputs, it will display a personalized message that includes the user's name and age.

We import the datetime module to get the current year. Then, we calculate the birth year by subtracting the age provided by the user from the current year. The program then displays the user's name, age, and the year they were born on.

Built-in Functions in Python

Python comes with a variety of built-in functions that provide essential functionalities to perform common tasks:

```python
# Using built-in functions for
common operations
print( abs( -5 ) ) # Output: 5
print( len( [1, 2, 3, 4] ) ) # Output:
4
print( max( 10, 20, 5 ) ) # Output: 20
print( min( 10, 20, 5 ) ) # Output: 5
```

output:

```
5
4
20
5
```

In this example, we showcase a few built-in functions:

- abs(): Returns the absolute value of a number.
- len(): Returns the length of a sequence (e.g., list, string).
- max(): Returns the maximum value from a sequence of arguments.
- min(): Returns the minimum value from a sequence of arguments.

These built-in functions are readily available in Python, saving you time and effort by eliminating the need to write these operations from scratch.

Volume Calculator

Here's a program that calculates the volume of different geometric shapes, including a cube and a sphere:

```python
import math

def cube_volume(side_length):
    return side_length ** 3

def sphere_volume(radius):
    return (4 / 3) * math.pi * radius ** 3

def main():
    print("Volume Calculator")
    print("1. Cube")
    print("2. Sphere")
    choice = input("Enter the number corresponding to the shape you want to calculate the volume for: ")

    if choice == "1":
        side_length = float(input("Enter the side length of the cube: "))
        volume = cube_volume(side_length)
        print(f"The volume of the cube is: {volume:.2f}")
    elif choice == "2":
        radius = float(input("Enter the radius of the sphere: "))
        volume = sphere_volume(radius)
        print(f"The volume of the sphere is: {volume:.2f}")
    else:
        print("Invalid choice. Please enter either '1' or '2'.")

if __name__ == "__main__":
    main()
```

In this program, the user can choose between calculating the volume of a cube or a sphere. Based on their choice, the program prompts the user for the necessary measurements (side length for the cube or radius for the sphere) and calculates the volume accordingly.

Python Tip 23

Type Conversion in Python

Type conversion, also known as typecasting, allows you to convert data from one type to another in Python.

Integer to String Conversion:

```python
age = 25 # Integer
age_str = str(age) # Convert integer to string
print("Age: " + age_str) # Output: "Age: 25"
```

output:
```
Age: 25
```

String to Integer Conversion:

```python
num_str = "10" # String num_int =
int(num_str) # Convert string to
integer result = num_int * 2
print(result) # Output: 20
```

output:
```
20
```

In these examples, we demonstrate converting between integer and string types using the str() and int() functions, respectively.

Type conversion is essential when you need to use data of a different type than the original. Python provides various functions for conversions, such as **int()**, **float()**, **str()**, **list()**, **tuple()**, and more, to handle different data types effectively.

Word Count

Here's a simple program that counts the number of words in a given sentence:

```python
def word_count(sentence):
    words = sentence.split()
    return len(words)

def main():
    print("Word Count")
    sentence = input("Enter a sentence: ")

    count = word_count(sentence)
    print(f"The sentence contains {count} words.")

if __name__ == "__main__":
    main()
```

Output:
```
Word Count
Enter a sentence: This is a simple sentence.
The sentence contains 5 words.
```

In this program, the user is prompted to enter a sentence. The word_count function then splits the sentence into individual words using the split method, and the length of the resulting list of words gives us the word count.

Python Tip 24

Logical Operators in Python

Logical operators (and, or, not) are used to combine or modify conditions in Python to make more complex and meaningful expressions.

and:
```python
num = 15
# Check if num is greater than 10 and
less than 20
if num > 10 and num < 20:
    print("The number is between 10 and
20.")
```

or:
```python
age = 15
# Check if age is either less than 18
or greater than 65
if age < 18 or age > 65:
    print("You are either too young or
too old for this activity.")
```

not:
```python
is_raining = False
# Check if it's not raining
if not is_raining:
    print("It's not raining, so you can
go outside.")
```

In these examples, we demonstrate how to use logical operators to combine conditions. The and operator requires both conditions to be true for the overall expression to be true. The or operator requires at least one condition to be true for the expression to be true. The not operator negates the truth value of a condition.

Xmas Tree

Here's a simple program that prints a Christmas tree ASCII art:

```python
def print_tree(height):
    for i in range(1, height + 1):
        spaces = " " * (height - i)
        stars = "*" * (2 * i - 1)
        print(spaces + stars)

def main():
    print("Christmas Tree")
    height = int(input("Enter the
height of the tree: "))
    print_tree(height)

if __name__ == "__main__":
    main()
```

Output:
```
Christmas Tree
Enter the height of the tree:  5
    *
   ***
  *****
 *******
*********
```

In this program, the user is prompted to enter a sentence. The word_count function then splits the sentence into individual words using the split method, and the length of the resulting list of words gives us the word count.

Nested Loops in Python

Nested loops involve using one loop inside another, allowing you to iterate over elements in a more complex structure:

```python
# Nested loops to create a
multiplication table
for i in range(1, 6):
    for j in range(1, 6):
        result = i * j
        print(f"{i} * {j} = {result}")
```

output:
```
1 * 1 = 1
1 * 2 = 2
~
5 * 4 = 20
5 * 5 = 25
```

In this example, we use nested loops to create a multiplication table from 1 to 5. The outer loop (for i in range(1, 6)) iterates over the first factor, and the inner loop (for j in range(1, 6)) iterates over the second factor. The result of each multiplication is printed in the format "1 * 1 = 1", "1 * 2 = 2", and so on.

Nested loops are useful for handling multidimensional data structures, traversing matrices, or performing iterative calculations. However, be cautious with deeply nested loops, as they can lead to performance issues in larger data sets.

Yes or No

Here's a simple program that asks the user yes or no questions and responds accordingly:

```python
def ask_yes_or_no(question):
    while True:
        answer = input(question + " (yes/no): ").lower()
        if answer == "yes":
            return True
        elif answer == "no":
            return False
        else:
            print("Please enter 'yes' or 'no'.")

def main():
    print("Yes or No Game")
    question = "Do you like pizza?"
    if ask_yes_or_no(question):
        print("Great! I like pizza too!")
    else:
        print("Oh, that's too bad. Pizza is delicious!")

if __name__ == "__main__":
    main()
```

Output:
```
Yes or No Game
Do you like pizza? (yes/no):  yes
Great! I like pizza too!
```

In this program, the ask_yes_or_no function repeatedly asks the user the given question until they provide a valid "yes" or "no" response. The main function uses this function to ask the user if they like pizza and responds accordingly based on their answer.

Python Tip 26

Enumerate in Python

The enumerate() function in Python is a powerful tool that simplifies looping by providing both the index and value of elements in a sequence:

```python
fruits = ["apple", "banana", "cherry"]

# Looping with enumerate to get index
and value
for index, fruit in enumerate(fruits):
    print(f"Index: {index}, Fruit:
{fruit}")
```

output:
```
Index: 0, Fruit: apple
Index: 1, Fruit: banana
Index: 2, Fruit: cherry
```

In this example, we use enumerate() to loop through the fruits list and obtain both the index and value of each element in the list. This helps avoid the need for manually managing a separate index variable.

The syntax of enumerate() is straightforward, and it improves the readability and simplicity of your code when you need to access both the index and value of elements in a loop.

Take advantage of the enumerate() function when iterating over lists, tuples, strings, or any other sequence in Python.

Zodiac Sign

A program that asks for the user's birthdate and shows their zodiac sign:

```python
def get_zodiac_sign(month, day):
    zodiac_signs = [
        ("Capricorn", (1, 1), (1, 19)),
("Aquarius", (1, 20), (2, 18)), ("Pisces",
(2, 19), (3, 20)),
        ("Aries", (3, 21), (4, 19)),
("Taurus", (4, 20), (5, 20)), ("Gemini",
(5, 21), (6, 20)),
        ("Cancer", (6, 21), (7, 22)),
("Leo", (7, 23), (8, 22)), ("Virgo", (8,
23), (9, 22)),
        ("Libra", (9, 23), (10, 22)),
("Scorpio", (10, 23), (11, 21)),
("Sagittarius", (11, 22), (12, 21)),
        ("Capricorn", (12, 22), (12, 31))
    ]

    return next((sign for sign,
(start_month, start_day), (end_month,
end_day) in zodiac_signs
                if (month == start_month
and day >= start_day) or (month ==
end_month and day <= end_day)), "Unknown")

def main():
    print("Zodiac Sign Determination")
    try:
        month, day = map(int, input("Please
enter your birthdate (MM/DD):
").split('/'))
        if 1 <= month <= 12 and 1 <= day <=
31:
            zodiac_sign =
get_zodiac_sign(month, day)
            print(f"Your zodiac sign is
{zodiac_sign}.")
        else:
            print("Invalid input. Please
enter a valid birthdate.")
    except ValueError:
        print("Invalid input. Please enter
your birthdate in the format MM/DD.")

if __name__ == "__main__":
    main()
```

Python Tip27

Default Arguments in Python Functions

Python allows you to define default values for function parameters, making them optional during function calls:

```python
# Function with default argument
def greet(name, greeting="Hello"):
    print(f"{greeting}, {name}!")

# Calling the function with both arguments
greet("Alice", "Hi")

# Calling the function with only one argument (uses default value)
greet("Bob")
```

output:
```
Hi, Alice!
Hello, Bob!
```

In this example, the function greet() has a default value for the greeting parameter set to "Hello". When you call the function with only one argument (greet("Bob")), it uses the default value for greeting and prints "Hello, Bob!".

Using default arguments enhances the flexibility and usability of your functions. It allows you to provide meaningful default values for certain parameters while still giving users the option to override those defaults when necessary.

Attack of the Monsters

In this game, the player will face a random monster and can choose to attack or defend:

```python
import random

def attack_player():
    return random.randint(5, 15)

def attack_monster():
    return random.randint(10, 20)

def main():
    player_health, monster_health = 100, 100

    print("Welcome to Attack of the Monsters!")
    print("You are facing a scary monster. You have
100 health points.")

    while player_health > 0 and monster_health > 0:
        print(f"Health: {player_health} | Monster
health: {monster_health}")
        print("1. Attack | 2. Defend")
        choice = input("Enter choice (1 or 2): ")

        if choice == "1":
            player_attack = attack_player()
            monster_damage = attack_monster()
            player_health -= monster_damage
            monster_health -= player_attack
            print(f"Attacked: -{monster_damage} |
You attacked: -{player_attack}")

        elif choice == "2":
            monster_attack = attack_monster() // 2
            player_health -= monster_attack
            print(f"Defended: -{monster_attack}")

        else:
            print("Wrong choice. Select 1 or 2.")

    if player_health <= 0:
        print("Oh no! You were defeated by the
monster. Game over.")
    else:
        print("Congratulations! You defeated the
monster. You are victorious!")

if __name__ == "__main__":
    main()
```

Python Tip28

Efficiently Generating Large Sequences

In Python, generator functions are a powerful way to create iterators and generate large sequences of data efficiently. Unlike regular functions that return a value and exit, generator functions use the yield keyword to yield data one element at a time. This makes them memory-efficient, especially when dealing with huge datasets or infinite sequences:

```python
def even_numbers(limit):
    for i in range(2, limit + 1, 2):
        yield i

# Using the generator to print even
numbers up to 10
print(list(even_numbers(10)))
```

output:
```
[2, 4, 6, 8, 10]
```

In this example, the even_numbers generator function yields even numbers from 2 up to the specified limit. Instead of generating all even numbers at once, it yields each number as needed. This is especially beneficial when dealing with large limit values, as it saves memory and processing time.

Monster Name Generator

Here's a small program to generate monster names:

```python
import random

def generate_monster_name():
    adjectives = ["Fierce", "Gigantic",
"Spooky", "Silly", "Gloomy", "Enormous",
"Playful", "Creepy"]
    animals = ["Dragon", "Yeti", "Goblin",
"Werewolf", "Kraken", "Griffin", "Ogre",
"Vampire"]

    adjective = random.choice(adjectives)
    animal = random.choice(animals)

    return f"{adjective} {animal}"

def main():
    print("Welcome to the Monster Name
Generator!")

    while True:
        input("Press Enter to generate a
monster name. Press Q to quit.")

        choice = random.random()

        if choice < 0.9:
            monster_name =
generate_monster_name()
            print(f"Your monster name is:
{monster_name}")
        else:
            print("Sorry, no monster name
generated this time.")

        if input("Would you like to generate
another monster name? (y/n): ").lower() !=
"y":
            break

if __name__ == "__main__":
    main()
```

This program generates monster names by
combining random adjectives with animal names.

Recursion in Python

Recursion is a powerful technique in programming where a function calls itself to solve a problem. It allows you to break complex problems into simpler, repetitive subproblems:

```python
# Recursive function to calculate the
factorial of a number
def factorial(n):
    if n == 0 or n == 1:
        return 1
    else:
        return n * factorial(n - 1)
# Calculate factorial of 5
result = factorial(5)
print(result)  # Output: 120
```

output:
120

In this example, we define a recursive function factorial() to calculate the factorial of a given number n. The base case is when n is 0 or 1, in which case the function returns 1. Otherwise, it recursively calls itself with n - 1 until reaching the base case.

Recursion is a powerful technique for solving certain problems, but it's essential to handle base cases correctly to avoid infinite loops. When using recursion, make sure to provide a well-defined base case to terminate the recursive calls.

Monster Catcher

Here's a small program to catch monsters:

```python
import random

def generate_monster():
    monsters = ["Goblin", "Ghost",
"Werewolf", "Vampire", "Dragon", "Zombie"]
    monster = random.choice(monsters)
    return monster

def catch_monster(player_name):
    monster = generate_monster()
    print(f"A wild {monster} appears!")
    response = input(f"{player_name}, do
you want to catch the {monster}? (yes/no):
").lower()

    if response == "yes":
        print(f"Congratulations, you caught
the {monster}!")
    else:
        print(f"The {monster} got away.
Better luck next time!")

def main():
    print("Welcome to Monster Catcher!")

    player_name = input("Enter your name:
")

    while True:
        catch_monster(player_name)

        play_again = input("Do you want to
play again? (yes/no): ").lower()
        if play_again != "yes":
            break

    print("Thanks for playing!")

if __name__ == "__main__":
    main()
```

Different monsters will randomly appear, and
the player has the option to catch them or let
them go. The game continues until the player
decides to stop. Enjoy catching those monsters!

List Slicing in Python

List slicing allows you to extract sublists and create new lists using a specific range or stride:

```python
# Original list
numbers = [0, 1, 2, 3, 4, 5, 6, 7, 8, 9]

# Extract a sublist from index 2 to 5 (exclusive)
sublist = numbers[2:5]
print(sublist)

# Create a new list with every second element
stride_list = numbers[::2]
print(stride_list)
```

output:
```
[2, 3, 4]
[0, 2, 4, 6, 8]
```

In this example:
- numbers[2:5] extracts a sublist from index 2 to 5 (exclusive), which includes elements [2, 3, 4].
- numbers[::2] creates a new list with every second element (stride of 2), resulting in [0, 2, 4, 6, 8].

List slicing is for manipulating lists efficiently. Allows you to work with specific parts of a list without modifying the original list. You can use list slicing to do operations, filtering elements, reversing lists, and extracting portions of a list.

Monster Transformation

Here's a simple Python program for Monster Metamorphosis:

```python
import random

def transform_name(name):
    prefixes = ['Zog', 'Grim', 'Fang',
'Snarl', 'Thorn', 'Claw']
    suffixes = ['zilla', 'moth',
'fang', 'ling', 'munch', 'claw']

    prefix = random.choice(prefixes)
    suffix = random.choice(suffixes)

    return prefix + name + suffix

def main():
    print("Welcome to Monster
Metamorphosis!")
    name = input("Please enter your
name: ")
    monster_name = transform_name(name)
    print("Your monster name is:",
monster_name)

if __name__ == "__main__":
    main()
```

This program defines a function transform_name() that takes a name as input and randomly combines it with a prefix and a suffix to create a unique monster name.

The main() function welcomes the user, takes their name as input, and then calls the transform_name() function to generate the monster name. Finally, the program prints out the monster name for the user to see.

Python Tip 31

String Formatting with f-strings

f-strings are a powerful way to create dynamic output by embedding expressions directly within strings:

```python
name = "Alice"
age = 30

# Using f-string for dynamic output
message = f"My name is {name} and I am {age} years old."
print(message)
```

output:

```
My name is Alice and I am 30 years old.
```

In this example, the f-string allows us to embed variables name and age directly within the string, making it easy to create dynamic output based on the values of these variables.

f-strings are a concise and readable way to format strings in Python. They support a wide range of expressions, including arithmetic, function calls, and even inline conditions. This makes f-strings a powerful tool for creating complex and dynamic output.

To use f-strings, simply prefix the string with the letter f, and then enclose expressions or variables in curly braces {}.

Monster Fortune Teller

Here's a simple Python program for fun monster-related fortunes:

```python
import random

def get_monster_fortune():
    monster_fortunes = [
        "A friendly ghost will bring you good luck.",
        "Beware of werewolves on the next full moon.",
        "Zombies may be clumsy, but you will find unexpected success.",
        "A mischievous vampire will play a trick on you.",
        "A helpful monster will assist you in a time of need.",
        "The Loch Ness Monster has hidden a surprise for you.",
        "A cute yeti will bring joy.",
        "Watch out for sneaky goblins trying to steal your snacks.",
        "A dragon will protect you.",
        "A sweet monster will surprise you with a gift.",
    ]
    return random.choice(monster_fortunes)

def main():
    print("The Monster Fortune Teller!")
    print("Press Enter to receive your fortune.")
    print("Press Q to quit.")

    while True:
        key = input()
        if key.lower() == "q":
            break

        print(get_monster_fortune())

if __name__ == "__main__":
    main()
```

Randomly selects and displays monster related fortunes to predict the future.

Python Tip 32

Lambda and Map in Python

Lambda functions (anonymous functions) and the map() function can simplify function definitions and list transformations:

```python
# Using lambda to square numbers
square = lambda x: x ** 2

# Applying lambda to a list of numbers
numbers = [1, 2, 3, 4, 5]
squared_numbers = map(square, numbers)
print(list(squared_numbers))  # Output:
[1, 4, 9, 16, 25]
```

<u>output:</u>
```
[1, 4, 9, 16, 25]
```

In this example:

- We define a lambda function square to calculate the square of a number x.
- We use the map() function to apply the square lambda function to each element in the numbers list, creating a new list with the squared values.

Lambda functions are concise and useful for simple calculations or transformations. The **map()** function applies a given function to all items in an iterable and returns an iterator with the results.

Lambda and map provide an elegant way to perform quick operations on lists or iterables, saving you time and lines of code.

Monster Alphabet

Here's a alphabet program for using
ASCII art letters with monster names:

```python
def                         ():
    monster_alphabet = {
        'A': (r"""

  A
 A A
AAAAA
A   A
A   A
""", "Abominable Snowman"),

        'B': (r"""
BBBB
B  B
BBBB
B  B
BBBB
""", "Bigfoot"),

        'C': (r"""
 CCCC
C
C
C
 CCCC
""", "Chupacabra"),

        # Add more monster-themed letters here
    }

    while True:
        letter = input("Enter a letter (A-Z)
or 'quit' to exit: ").upper()
        if letter == 'QUIT':
            break
        elif letter in monster_alphabet:
            print(monster_alphabet[letter][0])
            print(monster_alphabet[letter][1])
        else:
            print(f"Sorry, no monster-themed
letter for '{letter}'")

def main():


if __name__ == "__main__":
    main()
```

Defines a dictionary monster_alphabet containing
monster-themed ASCII art and names.

Python Tip33

Custom Exception Messages and Handling Multiple Errors

In Python, use try, except, and raise to handle errors and provide informative messages for exceptions:

```python
# Custom exception for negative numbers
class NegativeNumberError(Exception):
    pass
# Function to calculate square root of a positive number
def calculate_square_root(number):
    if number < 0:
        raise NegativeNumberError("Error: Negative number not allowed!")
    return number ** 0.5
# Handling exceptions with try-except
try:
    result = calculate_square_root(-9)
except NegativeNumberError as e:
    print(e)
```

output:
Error: Negative number not allowed!

In this example:
- We define a custom exception NegativeNumberError.
- The calculate_square_root() function raises NegativeNumberError for negative numbers, along with a custom error message.
- The try-except block catches the exception and prints the error message.

Monster Escape Room

Here's a game where the player needs to solve one puzzle to escape the room:

```python
def escape_room():
    print("You are trapped in a room filled with monsters!")
    print("To escape, you must find the key hidden in one of the boxes.")

    monster_boxes = ["1", "2", "3"]
    key_location = "2"

    while True:
        print("Choose a box to open (1, 2, or 3):")
        choice = input()

        if choice == key_location:
            print("Congratulations! You found the key and escaped from the monsters!")
            break
        elif choice in monster_boxes:
            print("Oh no! You opened a box and a monster attacked you. Try again.")
        else:
            print("Invalid input. Please choose a box number (1, 2, or 3).")

def main():
    escape_room()

if __name__ == "__main__":
    main()
```

You can expand the game by adding more rooms with diverse puzzles and challenges.

P y t h o n   T i p 3 4

List Comprehension with Conditionals

List comprehensions with conditionals allow you to create compact and expressive lists based on specific conditions:

```python
# Create a list of even numbers from 1
to 10 using list comprehension
even_numbers = [x for x in range(1, 11)
if x % 2 == 0]
print(even_numbers)  # Output: [2, 4, 6,
8, 10]
```

output:
```
[2, 4, 6, 8, 10]
```

In this example, the list comprehension [x for x in range(1, 11) if x % 2 == 0] generates a list of even numbers from 1 to 10. The condition if x % 2 == 0 filters only the even numbers.

List comprehensions with conditionals are concise and effective for creating filtered lists, avoiding the need for explicit loops.

Monster Rock Paper Scissors

Here's a game where the player needs to solve one puzzle to escape the room:

```python
import random

def get_user_choice():
    return input("Enter your choice: Rock, Paper, Scissors: ").strip().lower()

def get_computer_choice():
    return random.choice(["rock", "paper", "scissors"])

def determine_winner(user_choice, computer_choice):
    if user_choice == computer_choice:
        return "It's a tie!"
    wins = {"rock": "scissors", "paper": "rock", "scissors": "paper"}
    return "You win!" if wins[user_choice] == computer_choice else "Monster wins!"

def main():
    print("Welcome to the Monster Rock Paper Scissors Game!")
    print("You are playing against a monster!")

    while True:
        user_choice = get_user_choice()
        if user_choice == "quit":
            break

        computer_choice = get_computer_choice()

        print(f"Monster chose: {computer_choice}")

    print(determine_winner(user_choice, computer_choice))
        print()

if __name__ == "__main__":
    main()
```

Python Tip35

Using the zip() Function

The zip() function pairs elements from multiple lists together, allowing you to iterate over them simultaneously:

```python
names = ["Alice", "Bob", "Charlie"]
ages = [25, 30, 22]

# Zip names and ages together
for name, age in zip( names, ages ):
    print(f"{name} is {age} years old.")
```

output:
```
Alice is 25 years old.
Bob is 30 years old.
Charlie is 22 years old.
```

In this example, zip(names, ages) pairs the corresponding elements from the names and ages lists, allowing us to iterate over them together in the for loop.

The zip() function is handy when working with related data stored in separate lists, and it simplifies the process of combining information from multiple sources.

These additional Python tips will help you write more efficient and expressive code.

Monster Dice Game

Here's a simple Monster Dice Game:

```python
import random

def roll_dice():
    return random.randint(1, 6)

def monster_dice_game():
    print("Welcome to the Monster Dice
Game!")
    print("Roll the dice and see if you
can beat the monster.")

    while True:
        input("Press Enter to roll the
dice...")

        player_roll = roll_dice()
        monster_roll = roll_dice()

        print(f"You rolled:
{player_roll}")
        print(f"Monster rolled:
{monster_roll}")

        if player_roll > monster_roll:
            print("Congratulations! You
win!")
        elif player_roll < monster_roll:
            print("Oops! The monster
wins!")
        else:
            print("It's a tie!")

        play_again = input("Do you want
to play again? (y/n): ")
        if play_again.lower() != "y":
            break

if __name__ == "__main__":
    monster_dice_game()
```

The player and the monster each roll a dice,
and the one with the higher roll wins.

Python Tip 36

List comprehensions and dictionary comprehensions

Allow you to create lists and dictionaries in a concise and elegant way. They are a compact and Pythonic approach to generate new collections based on existing ones.

List Comprehension:

```python
# Regular way to create a list of
squares
numbers = [1, 2, 3, 4, 5]
squares = []
for num in numbers:
    squares.append(num ** 2)

# Using list comprehension
squares = [num ** 2 for num in numbers]
```

Dictionary Comprehension:

```python
# Regular way to create a dictionary
with squares as values
numbers = [1, 2, 3, 4, 5]
squares_dict = {}
for num in numbers:
    squares_dict[num] = num ** 2

# Using dictionary comprehension
squares_dict = {num: num ** 2 for num
in numbers}
```

Both list comprehensions and dictionary comprehensions are concise and easy to read. They can often replace the need for explicit loops and conditional statements.